HENRY JAMES

from a portrait of 1913 by J. S. SARGENT
National Portrait Gallery

HENRY JAMES

by

MICHAEL SWAN

PUBLISHED FOR
THE BRITISH COUNCIL
AND THE NATIONAL BOOK LEAGUE
BY LONGMANS, GREEN & CO

PS
2/23
S9
1969

LONGMANS, GREEN AND CO LTD
Longman House, Burnt Mill, Harlow, Essex

*Associated companies, branches and
representatives throughout the world*

First published 1950
Revised 1957
Reprinted with minor additions to text and Bibliography 1964
Revised 1969
© Michael Swan, 1957, 1969

*Printed in Great Britain by
F. Mildner & Sons, London, E.C.1*

HENRY JAMES

THE life and character of Henry James seem to have moved almost exactly in sympathy with the three 'periods' in his writing—those three periods which so many critics of James's work have called, 'James I, James II, and James the Old Pretender'. From the comparatively little material we have James I appears as a melancholy, heavy-eyed young man, shyly wandering Europe and passing whole seasons having spoken to few people other than chamber-maids and waiters. James II has found confidence and grown a beard; London is his home and he dines out four times a week; he is liked and admired, but something more grand is to come when he merges into the Old Pretender. The Legend of the Master (to echo the title of his story 'The Lesson of the Master') begins, and a man as extraordinary as his novels of this time is revealed. 'A quite lengendary figure,' wrote Hugh Walpole of him, 'a sort of stuffed waxwork from whose mouth a stream of coloured sentences, like rolls of green and pink paper, are for ever issuing.' Let us look closer at this legendary waxwork.

From the end of the 'nineties until his death James was one of the senior men of letters in England; he encouraged young writers with profound criticism, and among them his reputation was great, but even so he knew that wide popularity was something he could not hope for. 'Ah, Mr Jacobs, I envy you!' he said to W. W. Jacobs, the novelist and short-story writer, 'your admirable work is appreciated by a wide circle of readers; it has achieved popularity. Mine—never goes into a second edition. I should so much have loved to be popular.' This was after dinner at a London club and, if it were true to form, the evening would continue with a great deal of talk from James of an almost baroque complication. 'A ponderously warm manner of saying nothing in infinite sentences', was

Thomas Hardy's opinion, but others knew that when the design was complete it would have been well worth waiting for. Many accounts of his conversation have been written, but A. C. Benson's gives an excellent idea of its quality. 'The extreme and almost tantalizing charm of his talk lay not only in his quick transitions, his exquisite touches of humour and irony, the width and force of his sympathy, the range of his intelligence, but in the fact that the whole process of his thought, the qualifications, the resumptions, the interlineations were laid bare. The beautiful sentences, so finished, so deliberate, shaped themselves audibly upon the air. . . . He never strayed loosely, as most voluble talkers do, from subject to subject. The *motif* was precisely enunciated, revised, elongated, improved upon, enriched, but it was always, so to speak, strictly contrapuntal. . . . It was perfectly adjusted, delicately controlled.'

This gift of language, which came to maturity in him so late, was hereditary. Henry James senior was an American philosopher with an astonishing command of rhetoric, and in houses in New York, Albany and Boston, where Henry and his brother William (later to become the celebrated philosopher) spent most of their early years, conversation was almost continuous—with their father setting an example which they longed to emulate. It was one of the better aspects of the eccentric education which their father had chosen to give them. He wished to preserve their minds as *tabulae rasae* to receive whatever stamp their individual experience was to give them and he didn't want them to lose future time sweeping out 'the rubbish'. It was to be a moral and spiritual education, liberal and as eclectic as possible. They went to schools in America, France, Germany, and Switzerland, and although 'learning' was far from the first thing expected from them Henry James looked back on the succession of educational experiments without regret because they had stimulated the free play of curiosity and consciousness.

It was this early knowledge of Europe and European

languages which no doubt decided the kind of writer he was to become. He was an American, of Irish antecedents, but America seemed to him a continent too immature for the production of great literature, while Europe was ancient and ripe with tradition; it also represented for him that romantic 'otherness' which seemed to be so necessary to him as an artist. Consequently in 1869, after a short period at Harvard Law School where he understood 'nothing', he left for Europe. He was homesick in England and found London and Paris sordid. Rome 'beat everything' however and the effect was 'something indescribable'. For the next few months he saturated himself—the word became a favourite with him—in Italy, until its 'picturesqueness' made him want to go 'strongly' into political economy or the New England school system. But Europe had got him in thrall and he knew that it had a quality with which the great, rough America could never compete. Paris was the town whose intellectual and social influence he needed most and in 1875, the year after writing his first novel, *Roderick Hudson*, which is set in Italy, he arrived in Paris on his first visit as a professional man of letters. But how closed the literary and social worlds were, how defensive of any new-comers who might impair their perfect symmetry. Flaubert read his stories and called them '*proprement écrit*' but lacking in colour, and Turgeniev, more than the other lions, took notice of him. But he wanted to have a closer association with this group of writers whose work he admired so much —except in one way. His Puritanism, which in America had seemed almost non-existent in comparison with that around him, became more apparent in France. He wrote of the modern French novel, 'Everything ran to form, and the successful books were apt to resemble little vases, skilfully moulded and chiselled, into which unclean things had been dropped.' He was himself to use many immoral themes in his own books, but it was the treatment rather than the use of such themes which shocked him.

At the end of his year in Paris he knew that he had 'lost',

and the uninformativeness of his letters at this time perhaps reveals his anxiety that his New England friends, who disapproved of his abjectness to Europe, should not know of her failure. Paris had taught him a great deal and he would always return to her with love—'I have loved France as I have never loved a woman', he once told a friend—and he would correspond regularly with his French friends; Paris would always be there to give him a refreshing sense of being able to get away from whatever place he decided should be his home. That place, he was almost sure, would be London—and the siege of London was begun. In London he was to find the Europe which did not, like France and Italy, 'keep holding one at arm's length, and condemning one to a meagre scraping of the surface'. He wrote to his mother at the end of his first few months there: 'I take very kindly to London, and am immensely contented at having come here. I must be a born Londoner for the place to stand the very severe test I am putting it; leaving Paris and its brilliances and familiarities, its easy resources and the abundant society I had there, to plunge into darkness, solitude and sleet, in mid-winter, to say nothing of the sooty, woolly desolation of a London lodging—to do that, and to like this murky Babylon really all the better is to feel that one is likely to get on here. . . . I find it interesting, inspiring, even exhilarating.' It was to be his home to the end of his life, although it was only an upsurge of passionate love for England at the outbreak of the 1914 war which made him become a British citizen.

The choice was made—for the old world. It was more than his choice, it was his need and his life—'and with that new world, *je n'ai que faire*'. He was now ready to write his novels of the 'international situation' in which he hoped that his readers would be unable to tell whether he was an American writing with knowledge about English people or an Englishman writing with knowledge about Americans. He was detached in England—and would certainly have been so in America—and set about the problem of 'knowing' England in a way the English could never know it. His books, letters and notebooks show how completely he came to know England, but they also reveal him becoming more and more an Englishman, sharing in those taboos and conventions in which, during his first years in England, he had no more than a detached interest. One cannot imagine him, for instance, writing the following in his later years: 'The condition of that body (the English upper classes) seems to me in many ways very much in the same rotten and *collapsible* one as that of the French aristocracy before the revolution—minus cleverness and conversation.' This passage supports the feeling which much of James's work gives that he is a gentle prophet of dissolution. The world of leisure and wealth which is the usual world of his novels is drawing towards its end, and it must have been his Puritanical side which seemed to sense an odour of corruption, almost of evil, about this world which his more hedonistic side admired and whose pleasures it adored.

By the late eighties he had become tired of the 'international situation' mainly because he was more *en rapport* with English than with American life and the novels of his second period are set in Europe, and, usually, with English characters. But for the first five years of the 'nineties he wrote no novels; he had begun his great and unrequited flirtation with the drama. Remembering his remark to W. W. Jacobs that he would have 'loved to be popular' one may see here a reason for this experiment. His popularity at this time had declined and he felt that a great theatrical success would restore it. He enjoyed the problems of the dramatic form, and *The American* had a moderate success; but the reception of *Guy Domville* made him decide to end this 'sawdust and orange peel' phase. He retired to a house at Rye, in Sussex, and returned to novel-writing, but with a new technique which was largely influenced by his work for the theatre. The air-tight structure, the mastery of 'fundamental statement' and the wish to produce a novel 'all dramatic, all scenic' are the characteristics of the later style—and are all requisite in the theatre.

The last years of his life we have already glimpsed at, and such a glimpse is probably more revealing than an account of the events of those years, which were as serene as the occupations of his mind must have been turbulent; for he was experiencing a period of almost visionary inspiration, a period which one might compare to the last great years of Beethoven or of Turner. But one event was important—his visit to America in 1903. He had long delayed the visit, knowing how formidable the return after so many years would be. He summed up his visit with the following words: 'I found my native land, after so many years, interesting, formidable, fearsome, and fatiguing, and much more difficult to see and deal with in any extended and various way than I had supposed. . . . I found many of the conditions too deterrent . . . it is an extraordinary world, an altogether huge proposition . . . but almost cruelly charmless, in effect, and calculated to make one crouch, ever afterwards as cravenly as possible, at Lamb House, Rye—if one happens to have a poor little L.H., R. to crouch in.' He wrote a book of impressions, *The American Scene*, and a few stories followed which 'came out' of his visit. Some years later he began an 'American' novel, *The Ivory Tower*, but this was discontinued at the outbreak of war.

In June 1915 he decided to take out papers of naturalization. At the declaration of war he had become immediately intensely patriotic towards England, a feeling partly explained by his dislike for Germany and all things German. Logan Pearsall Smith describes him at a luncheon party given by Edith Wharton: ' . . . into the room he burst, his great eyes ablaze. "My hands, I must wash them!" he cried. "My hands are dripping with blood. All the way from Chelsea to Grosvenor Place I have been bayoneting, my dear Edith, and hurling bombs, and ravishing and raping. It is my day-dream to squat down with King George of England, with the President of the French Republic and the Czar of Russia on the Emperor William's belly, until we squeeze out of it the last irrevocable drops of bitter retribution." ' After he had become a British citizen it pleased him to say that he had done so in order to be able to say 'We' when he talked about an 'Advance'.

On 1 January 1916 he was given the Order of Merit and on 28 February of the same year he died. On his memorial tablet he is described as a 'lover and interpreter of the fine amenities, of brave decisions and generous loyalties'.

Henry James wrote twenty-one novels and in the space of this essay it would be impossible to write of them all. I have therefore dealt in some detail with three novels which best represent his three periods. Every critic would probably vary in his choice of these three, but for my purpose I have chosen *Roderick Hudson* (1876), *The Portrait of a Lady* (1881) and *The Golden Bowl* (1904). They seem very clearly to mark his progression in subject matter, in style, and, above all, in technique—the change from the simple statement of thought and feeling to the subtlest, most tenuous expression of states of mind, which few novelists before James had attempted.

When he wrote *Roderick Hudson* James was still an American tourist in Europe, wandering round France and Italy and taking in 'the picturesque' in ample gulps. But something else beside these visual beauties began to occupy his mind. To his friend Grace Norton he wrote ' . . . it proves that even a creature addicted as much as I am over the whole *mise en scène* of Italian life, doesn't find an easy initiation into what lies behind'. For him what lay behind he came to call 'the international situation.' In its rudiments it was the impact of Europe on Americans, the old on the new, of experience on innocence. The possibilities of permutation on this situation were endless.

In those early years he saw Europe very plainly as a place for the moral destruction of the innocent New Worlders who visited it, the returning Puritans who had no idea of the world from which their ancestors had departed. Here, James saw, was drama, and he began to write *Roderick*

Hudson. A wealthy American discovers Roderick, a sculptor of promise, working in an office in a small Massachusetts town, and takes him to Italy to study. Roderick leaves a fiancée behind and a mother, both of whom believe that he will not like the ease of European life. Instead his genius flowers in the new climate—but a genius which he dissipates by falling too easily into the pleasure-loving ways of Europe. He doesn't work, his amatory affairs take up much of his time, and he has become the kind of complicated creature Massachusetts would know nothing of. At this point he falls in love with the beautiful Christina Light, whose mother is travelling with her round Europe in search of a good match. Christina is anything but innocent and tortures Roderick into further dissipation which culminates in his death fall from an Alpine peak.

Roderick Hudson is an extremely American novel. It would have been impossible for a European novelist of this period to have thought of the theme of the book, let alone to have written it. On the other hand no American novelist could have written it without a knowledge of Europe. It must be admitted, however, that James's idea of Europe in this book is a little naïve. His Puritanism, his own innocence in fact, comes out in his conception of Europe as a kind of wicked paradise; but the theme of the novel is important; it has a vital point of view, and in general has a right to a rather higher regard than it is usually allowed. The point of view was something of great importance for James the man and the artist, since his relationship to Europe was what occupied, and was to continue to occupy, his mind. He 'felt' *Roderick Hudson* in a way he had felt none of his previous work. There is a passage in which the whole matter of the book is stated with a delicacy and symbolism more characteristic of the later books. Rowland Mallet, Roderick's patron, is looking at Roderick's statuette of a boy with a cup:

'Tell me,' said Rowland, 'do you mean anything by your young Waterdrinker? Does he represent an idea? Is he a symbol?' Hudson raised his eyebrows and gently scratched his head. 'Why, he's a youth you know; he's innocence, he's health, he's curiosity. Yes, he's a good many things.' 'And is the cup also a symbol?' 'The cup is knowledge, pleasure, experience. Anything of that kind!'

It was a first novel and the importance of the theme is not sufficient to permit us to overlook its weaknesses. Roderick himself is conceived as a full-length portrait, one of the few full-length portraits in James's work, but what is achieved in fullness is lost in other ways, for Roderick is not memorable, and in spite of his charm, is not sympathetic. We are told that he is a great sculptor, but he gives little indication of any greatness of character. James seems to apprehend him only from the outside, and although he is full of 'information' about him he seems unwilling or unable to give him 'in the round', to use Mr E. M. Forster's phrase in differentiating between 'round' and 'flat' characters in fiction. His disintegration is the centre-piece of the novel, but it is handled with an inappropriate delicacy. His more vicious pursuits invariably take place off-stage, a method which the later James succeeded in making more horribly suggestive than anything which could have taken place on-stage; but here it seems to be the result of James's own inexperience in such matters. The disintegration takes place at a quite alarming rate, and the slow, agonizing process of decay is speeded up so much that the effect is lost. In later years James himself was aware of this weakness saying that although Roderick was necessarily a 'special case' (and how he loved special cases) he was not so special that he could disintegrate in a matter of weeks. Christina Light is perhaps the best-drawn character in the book, she is beautiful, mysterious in her origins, brilliant and capable of any eccentricty of behaviour. James enjoyed her so much that he put her into a later novel, *The Princess Casamassima*.

In *Roderick Hudson* James for the first time discovered the novelist's perpetual problem—the precise method by which life, which is flowing and continuous, may be cut into lengths while retaining the illusion of continuity. In the following quotation James considers this problem, and the whole passage is worth quoting, since the thought it contains underlies all his work:

Really, universally, relations stop nowhere, and the exquisite problem of the artist is eternally but to draw, by a geometry of his own, the circle within which they shall happily *appear* to do so. He is in the perpetual predicament that the continuity of things is the whole matter, for him, of comedy and tragedy; that this continuity is never, by the space of an instant or an inch, broken, and that, to do anything at all, he has at once intensely to consult and intensely to ignore it. All of which will perhaps pass for a supersubtle way of pointing the plain moral that a young embroiderer of the canvas of life soon began to work in terror, fairly, of the vast expanse of that surface, of the boundless number of its distinct perforations for the needle, and of the tendency inherent in his many-coloured flowers and figures to cover and consume as many as possible of the little holes. The development of the flower, of the figure, involved thus an immense counting of holes and a careful selection among them. That would have been, it seemed to him, a brave enough process, were it not the very nature of the holes so to invite, to solicit, to persuade, to practice positively a thousand lures and deceits. The prime effect of so sustained a system, so prepared a surface, is to lead on and on; while the fascination of following resides, by the same token, in the presumability *somewhere* of a convenient, of a visibly-appointed stopping place. Art would be easy indeed if, by a fond power disposed to 'patronize' it, such conveniences, such simplifications, had been provided. We have, as the case stands, to invent and establish them, to arrive at them by a difficult, dire process of selection and comparison, of surrender and sacrifice. The very meaning of expertness is acquired courage to brace one's self for the cruel crisis from the moment one sees it grimly loom.

The 'young embroiderer' was James himself at the time of his writing *Roderick Hudson*, and the methods by which the immature James tackled the difficulties so well set out above are interesting and almost successful. He could not put in everything, and mere elimination was too simple an alternative. Instead he chose to have an 'observer', a man not directly involved in the drama, but intensely interested in it, a sensitive mind through which the drama may be seen; in this way the illusion of completeness could be kept while, in fact, a rigid selection was being practised. The observer is Rowland Mallet, Roderick's patron. James constantly used this device, and although he used it better than in *Roderick Hudson*, the plan modestly succeeds. The book is realistic and relations are made to appear happily to end. There is something of Balzac in the way James builds up his characters, his situations, and all that appertains to his characters in the given situations, by this pattern of acutely observed details. Balzac, at this time, was James's avowed master.

Roderick Hudson has blemishes, but altogether it is a fine example of the traditional novel, with a well-developed plot and a wealth of incidental action and colour; everthing is clear, everything is logical, and in only one thing does James depart from what was accepted at the time as the only pattern for the novel. His unhappy ending was not liked, and one of the reasons why his novels were never popular was that he invariably chose a tragic ending. He always admitted that his novels were not designed to give his readers 'agreeable aftertastes'.

By 1881, when he published *The Portrait of a Lady*, James had mastered the technique of the novel, and any blemishes ceased to be obvious. This novel has always been recognized as the best novel of the middle period, but of recent years a school of thought has been active in claiming it as his finest novel. The distinguished critic, Dr F. R. Leavis, has said that 'something went wrong' with James as a novelist, and, not altogether convincingly, argues that James was at his greatest during his middle period.

There are Americans in *The Portrait of a Lady*, but the international situation is not a preoccupation. The heroine is an American girl, Isobel Archer, perhaps the most perfectly realized of all James's heroines. She is completely sympathetic—beautiful, charming, and morally incorruptible, without being a prig. Her creator describes her with the words: 'She spent half her time thinking of beauty, and bravery, and magnanimity; she had a fixed determination to regard the world as a place of brightness, of free expansion, of irresistible action. . . . She had an infinite hope that she would never do anything wrong.' In love with her is Lord Warburton, who symbolizes James's idea of the kind of English aristocrat who combines worldliness with intelligence, awareness of his position with sensitivity. Warburton and his world are shown to be admirable—no satire even is used to make Isobel's rejection of it appear to be anything more than it is, namely an instinct to 'find' herself in her own world. Unlike Roderick Hudson, Europe will not ensnare her. But she also rejects her other suitor, a worthy New Englander called Caspar Goodwood. Her world is not the rich provinciality of New England, but what it is neither the reader nor she herself precisely knows. This is the central motivation of the novel; she is innocently ready for an insidious approach. This comes in the form of Mme Merle and Gilbert Osmond, the former a *femme du monde* who knows 'none but the best people', the latter an impoverished gentleman of great charm who spends his days tending his collection of *objets d'art* in a Florentine villa. Isobel falls in love with him, and the reader wonders how she is able to be taken in by a man whose insincerity is so obviously not outweighed by his charm. But it is a point of great subtlety in James's conception of the novel that the reason is here vague, that Isobel's goodness will not easily allow her to see defect, while her innocence makes her an easy victim. For she is literally, a victim; Osmond and Mme Merle are lovers, and the marriage has been arranged in order to provide their daughter Pansy with a dowry. But, seeing only nobility in him, Isobel is certain that she has at last found the world in which she may develop without a radical change.

Inevitably the great disillusion follows, she discovers all the deceptions and realizes the true character of her husband. It is an immense climax and James himself must have thought long over the kind of actions which could possibly result from it. It is the test of her character; her wish to behave morally might force her to punish in any fit way these people who have involved her in their schemes, but her wish to regard the world with magnanimity may suggest forgiveness. She does, in fact, leave her husband, and she learns that Casper Goodwood still wishes to marry her. Yet, deliberately, quite consciously accepting her fate, she returns to Osmond; a woman, apparently made for nothing but happiness, condemns herself to a life which cannot be happy, because she has been made aware of 'what people most know and suffer'. But that explanation does not entirely satisfy and, indeed, no explanation of this strange action can satisfy. It is best not to be logical, but to ask whether, in the given circumstances, it is possible for a woman such as Isobel to return to Osmond. James convinces one that this is a special case and possible. It is only after the book has been laid down that doubt comes and we start applying logical reasoning to human behaviour. It is this delayed action doubt which makes many readers wonder, after having finished reading *The Portrait of a Lady*, whether it is as fine a novel as they have imagined it to be during the actual reading of it.

It was in this novel that James first completely broke away from the traditional manner of novel-writing. *Roderick Hudson* is a straightforward piece of story-telling, but in *The Portrait of a Lady* he wrote, so to speak, on two planes; he told a story full of significant action almost entirely in terms of the inner life of his protagonists. This method is more or less taken for granted by the modern novelist, but in 1881 it was an unnoticed revolution of technique. For this reason alone *The Portrait of a Lady* should be considered a book of great importance in the history of the novel.

It will be seen from the foregoing that what he called the 'international situation' was still present in James's mind, but it has been infinitely subtilized since the simple colours of *Roderick Hudson*. Only in the lesser characters such as

Henrietta Stackpole, the American journalist, and Lord Warburton are the differences between Europe and America simply expressed. In Isobel herself we are conscious of no particular country or continent (that, indeed, was her trouble). She is a person naturally detached from the roots of her own country. For this reason it is tempting to imagine that James put much of himself into her—and an argument could well be made out for this view. But although the means are subtler, James did show the same relationship between America and Europe in this novel as he had in *Roderick Hudson*; Isobel is an American and innocent; Mme Merle and Osmond, the European and the deracinated, teach her experience.

Five years after the publication of *The Portrait of a Lady* James published *The Bostonians* and *The Princess Casamassima*, neither of which deal with the international situation. In 1890 he published *The Tragic Muse*, which is almost entirely English in its setting and is, indeed, the most completely 'English' of all his novels. During the first half of the 'nineties he was occupied with playwriting; he had always been fascinated by the stage, but he was not a natural playwright and his dramatic career ended when his *Guy Domville* was mercilessly booed at the St James's Theatre in 1895.[1] Many years earlier (1878) Henry James had written a letter to William James: 'I am very impatient to get at work writing for the stage—a project I have long had. I am . . . certain I should succeed and it would be an open gate to money-

---

[1] After *Guy Domville*, six plays were written by James: *Summersoft* (One Act, 1895), *The High Bid* (Three Acts, 1907), Rough statement for Three Acts founded on *The Chaperon* (1907), *The Saloon* (One Act, 1908), *The Other House* (Scenario, 1893; Three Acts, 1908), *The Outcry* (Three Acts, 1909). *The High Bid* was produced in Edinburgh in 1908 and four matinee performances were given in London. The *Evening Standard* described the play as 'an afternoon of sheer delight' and the *Daily Chronicle* spoke of James as a dramatist 'inexpressibly delightful and incorrigibly impossible'. *The Saloon* opened in London in 1911. The *Daily Chronicle* said it was 'a distinct compliment to our stage', and the *Sunday Times* asked: 'Do people ever say such things and in such a manner?' *The Outcry* was produced by the Incorporated Stage Society, and performed twice in July 1917.

making.' Four years later the Madison Square Theatre rejected his dramatization of *Daisy Miller*. In his journal James writes: 'what it has brought (me) to know, both in New York and in London about the manners and ideas of managers and actors and about the conditions of productions on our unhappy stage, is almost fatally disgusting and discouraging. I have learned very vividly that if one attempts to work for it one must be prepared for *disgust* . . .' In a letter to his publisher, William Heinemann, he wrote: 'it is a most unholy trade!' In 1923, in a letter to the *Times Literary Supplement*, Bernard Shaw referred to 'the disastrous plays of James', his conclusion being that 'there is a literary language which is perfectly intelligible to the eye, yet utterly unintelligible to the ear even when it is easily speakable by the mouth . . . a writer who has always worked for publication alone is likely to fail in direct proportion to his inveterate practice and his virtuosity . . . But the disastrous plays of James, and the stage failures of novelists obviously much more richly endowed by nature and culture than many of the successful playwrights with whom they have tried to compete, suggest that they might have succeeded if only they had understood that as the pen and the *viva vox* are different instruments, their parts must be scored accordingly.' Granville-Barker disagreed with Shaw's view and referred to the dialogue, which he said 'is artificial— very; but that is legitimate. It might be hard to speak but I think that most of it could be made very effective once the right method had been found (I speak from memory of it) . . . Actors certainly could not blend it with 'melodramatic' acting: this was probably the fault with *The Saloon*—the incongruity. But I suggest to you to place it beside a Congreve and a Wycherley. It may not be so good as the first but I believe you'd find more style and bite in it than in the second.'

In 1896 he brought out *The Other House*, adapted from the play-scenario written in 1893. The influence of the stage now became apparent in all his work, in its economical construction and his awareness of the dramatic effect of climax. He said himself that the theatre had given him a 'mastery of fundamental statement', and all his novels were henceforth preceded by 'a really detailed scenario, intensely structural, intensely hinged and jointed preliminary frame'.

The novels of this time mark the beginning of the celebrated 'later manner' and they culminated in the publication of *The Wings of the Dove* (1902), *The Ambassadors* (1903) and *The Golden Bowl* (1904). In these novels he returned to the subject matter of the first period—the international situation —but with an entirely new equipment. He was now more European than American and he was aware that his knowledge of America and American life was out of date. But he was, even so, now ready to achieve his ambition of appearing to write from a sort of detached equipoise in mid-Atlantic. I have chosen to discuss *The Golden Bowl* at length because it most easily reveals aspects of James with which I am here dealing.

The protagonists of *The Golden Bowl* are Prince Amerigo, an improverished Italian, who marries Maggie Verver, the daughter of an American millionaire, for her money. This convenient marriage is prevented from being altogether distasteful by the fact that Amerigo admires and respects his wife, and has been brought up in a society where such marriages are not immoral. Amerigo has been the lover of Maggie's great friend Charlotte Stant, but they both decide that their liaison must end with the marriage. Maggie, thinking of her father's loneliness, invites Charlotte and her father to stay with them and, as she has hoped, Adam Verver marries Charlotte. The two couples are constantly with each other, and the delicate complications begin. Amerigo and Charlotte vow never to give in to their passion, to be entirely faithful. But at the very moment of this vow their passion overcomes them: 'Then of a sudden, through this tightened circle as at the issue of a narrow strait into the sea beyond, everything broke up, broke down, gave way, melted and mingled. Their lips sought their lips, their pressure their response and their response their pressure; with a violence that had sighed itself the next moment to the longest and deepest stillnesses they passionately sealed their pledge.' Maggie is innocent of the situation she is in; she discovers it accidentally through the buying of a golden bowl. The shopkeeper visits her to tell her that she has bought the bowl without knowing that it is cracked, and goes on to tell her of the visit, long before, of a pair of infatuated lovers who decided that a cracked bowl would bring bad luck if given as a wedding present. Maggie recognizes Amerigo and Charlotte from the description of the lovers, searches her married life for hints and suggestions whose significance she has not realized, and for the first time understands her situation. A friend visits her, hears the story, and immediately smashes the golden bowl on the floor, saying 'Whatever you meant by it—and I don't want to know *now*—has ceased to exist'. But the reader wonders whether the fate of the bowl will be symbolical of the events that follow. Maggie tells Amerigo that she knows everything, but there is no great scene; we are aware of the complications, of the suspicion and the torment which is going on in the minds of the quartet. But nothing is said, the intolerable atmosphere is suggested by an infinite weaving of delicate threads.

All behave as civilized people of the world, determined that an impulsive action shall not wreck their tenuous existence. A pattern of astonishing subtlety is drawn by James which culminates logically in reconciliation. To understand all is to forgive all—even if sacrifice is necessary, and it is Maggie's sacrifice which makes Amerigo's final love for her possible.

This long novel is a complete study of the permutations of the given situation; apart from the four protagonists there are no characters except an elderly couple who form the 'observing, detached eye' which James's methods demanded. Here, to a degree unimagined by the author of *Roderick Hudson* or even of *The Portrait of a Lady*, life has been shaped and moulded in order to describe a circle in which 'relations' may happily appear to end. Those who do not admire the later manner attack it for precisely these reasons, saying that life cannot be smoothed and moulded to the extent which James found necessary. They accuse him of being more interested in his technique than in his characters or his ideas, more concerned with contriving a beautiful shape to his novel than with searching the human heart. Even James's brother William, the philosopher, confessed himself bemused by the later style. While it is quite true that those novels show an immense interest in technique I cannot see that it is anything approaching a preoccupation. Their characters are admittedly not drawn 'in the round', they are not luscious and juicy, but only because they are not by nature luscious and juicy. They are people of an imagined and, for James, an ideal sensibility, and while it is not likely that in life such people would find themselves involved together in a situation, such a criticism has nothing to do with art. One need not go as far as saying with Gide that 'art only begins with the getting rid of Nature', but a glance at Aristotle provides the whole justification of the later style: 'The impossible, in general, is to be justified by referring either to the end of poetry itself, or to what is best, or to opinion. For with respect to poetry, impossibilities, rendered probable, are preferable to things improbable, though possible. With respect also to what is best, the imitation of poetry should resemble the paintings of Zeuxis; the example should be more perfect than nature.'

But to return to *The Golden Bowl*. We have again the familiar situation of Adam and Maggie, the pure innocents who become experienced in the hands of the European, Amerigo, and the mentally deracinated Charlotte. But, less than in *The Portrait of a Lady* is the America-Europe relationship in the forefront of James's mind. It is almost as if this relationship has become inevitable, the unconsidered accompaniment to so much of what he wrote. What, then, is the 'point of view' of the novel? I would say that James

had no more portentous an intention than to inquire minutely into the workings of four sensitive minds undergoing
certain disturbances, and by enquiring minutely into so
small a sphere of life to illuminate the whole. In the process
we are forced into considering the nature of passion, of
sacrifice and resignation, of evil, of integrity and innocence.
So far from seeking to escape from life, in his later manner
James was occupied with its very essence and he was able
to express his fleeting views of this essence perhaps more
adequately than any novelist before him. In order to express
this glimpsed vision a new language was needed, a language
as elusive and as subtle as the things he wished to express.
To accuse James of perverseness in forming his later style is
entirely to misunderstand its purpose; the ideas, not the
style, came first. This style was a formidable weapon which
he found himself able to master, but almost as if he wishes
to smile at himself he sometimes abuses this mastery. He
goes too far, the commas multiply, the parentheses burgeon
one upon the other, and we begin to think sympathetically
of H. G. Well's description of James as 'a hippopotamus
picking up a pea'. This is nowhere better shown than in a
letter to a friend, in 1912, thanking him for the present
of a suitcase:

Bonne renommée vaut mieux que sac-de-voyage doré, and though I may
have had weaknesses that have brought me a little under public notice,
my modest hold-all (which has accompanied me in most of my voyage
through life) has at least, so far as I know, never *fait jaser* . . . That you
conceivable (*quoi, à peine!*) but that you shouldn't have counted the cost
shouldn't have counted the cost—to yourself—that is after all perhaps
to *me*, to whom it spells ruin: *that* ranks you with those great lurid,
though lovely, romantic and historic figures and charmers who have
scattered their affections and lavished their favours only (as it has
presently appeared) to consume and to destroy!

The vein is continued for another 300 words.

The later style, for all its complexity, is loquitive, that is
to say it is a 'spoken' style. James, indeed, rarely actually
wrote in this style, since from 1896 onwards he cultivated

the habit of dictating to his secretary, after preparing a complete scenario of the novel; the dictation was then revised. And in normal social life he tended to speak in the same manner; at dinner parties all conversation would sometimes cease while his long periods slowly and painfully unwound themselves. Adjectives would be tried and discarded one by one until the *mot juste* was at last found.

Throughout his life Henry James wrote short stories, and a large proportion of his collected edition is devoted to the best of these stories, which vary from the short anecdote to the *nouvelle*. In a letter he once wrote that he delighted in 'deep-breathing economy and an organic form', and, as we have seen, the formal element was of first importance to him. The word 'economy', however, may sound rather strange, coming from James; his sentences have a way of never seeming to end, and nearly all his novels are very long. He means by economy that the structure of a story or a novel should be free of irrelevance, and his own stories have this quality. They explore a certain state of mind, or a situation, in an attempt to present it complete; he rarely concerns himself with sub-plots, or with more than one issue, and when one reads his notebooks one may see that the 'idea' for his stories usually came in the form of a short remark from a friend. The whole story was contained, unexplored, in this remark.

James's first published work was a short story, and many of these early stories were republished after his death. It is not certain that James would have approved of this, since they are not stories of great merit. They are melodramatic and lack all the psychological interest of the later work, and yet there is always a fascination in reading the prentice work of a great writer. 'The Romance of Certain Old Clothes' is among the better of these stories, and here, for the first time, appears that great interest which James had in the supernatural—and his desire to ally it with the natural. Probably the best example of the early stories, 'The Last of the Valerii', is concerned with a similar aim. In this story the

Count Valerio discovers a Juno in the garden of his villa near Rome—a statue of such beauty that he neglects his wife and spends his days contemplating her. It is only when the Juno is buried again that he can return to his wife. The supernatural is not explicit here, but we are conscious of some pagan power in this stone which acts on the mind of the count in a way which is almost supernatural. Yet there is a straining towards symbolism which does not wholly convince us that the story is expressing some truth; ultimately it seems to be little more than a beautifully told ghost story —a piece of 'bugaboo', to use James's own word. The idea of a living creature falling in love with an image of beauty seems to have fascinated him, and with a little courage one might say that it symbolizes his eventual departure from the everyday world of reality into a sort of impossible, ideal reality. There is an image of beauty in an early, and rather absurd, story called 'Rose Agathe', in which an antique collector rhapsodizes over the beauty of a hairdresser's wax model, and will not rest until he has bought her. And in 'The Special Type', a later story, Mrs Dundene buys the portrait of the man she loves but cannot have, saying, 'It will be *him* for me. I shall live with it, keep it all to myself'.

'The Last of the Valerii', except as a parable, has very little to do with 'life'. In his later years James pretended to despise life—she was so stupid, so clumsy—but it is clear that he never lost his interest in it. In his novel *The Ambassadors* the hero, Lambert Strether, has allowed 'life' to pass him by; one day he advises a young man to 'Live, Live!' It needs little imagination to see that this is really James himself wondering whether it is better to contemplate and understand life than to live it.

'The only reason for the existence of the novel is that it should attempt to represent life,' James once wrote, and some critics feel that he ceased to obey this injunction as he grew older. He knew that, once his *people* could no longer be related to the real world, this sentence would have lost all meaning for him. But his characters never lost their reality, becoming well observed, living people moving in a poetic world. In his story 'The Bench of Desolation' his protagonists are a lower middle-class man and woman, Herbert Dodd and Kate Cookham; they are presented almost photographically in their class—yet the idea of the story and the dream-like atmosphere which James induces could not be further from reality. The two are in love, but through a misunderstanding each believes that the other has ceased to love, and Herbert marries someone else. Kate brings an action for breach of promise, and all Herbert's money goes in settling the case. Years pass; he is unhappy, having lost his wife and gone bankrupt; he takes to sitting on a bench on the Marine Parade of a seaside town, where he had once courted Kate. One day Kate approaches him on the bench, and he learns that she has always loved him, and that she has kept the money she won in the action, knowing that one day he would need both it and her.

In this wonderful story James has not allowed 'clumsy life to get at her stupid work'. Outlined as an anecdote the story seems false, a little absurd; if there are people to be found who act so idiotically why write about them? Yet James has transformed this material into a profound and moving reflection on life and human nature—a particle of truth is offered and accepted. A quotation from the end of the story will show something of its quality. The passion we are conscious of between the two ageing lovers as they sit on the bench is suggested by that inarticulately eloquent dialogue of which James is such a master. And then, in the last sentence, there is the first physical touch: 'He leaned forward, dropping his elbows to his knees, and pressing his head on his hands. So he stayed, saying nothing; only with a sense of her own sustained, renewed and wonderful action, knowing that an arm had been passed round him and that he was held. She was beside him on the bench of desolation.' It is remarkable how affecting and deeply passionate those few quiet sentences are.

I have been speaking here of the very serious stories,

among which may also be included 'The Altar of the Dead', 'The Beast in the Jungle', and 'The Jolly Corner'. The lighter stories, like 'The Beldonald Holbein', 'The Real Thing', or 'The Velvet Glove', may not be so moving but their pre-occupations are similar. 'The Real Thing', for instance, is an ironic playing with the old theme of reality, in which an artist discovers that he can draw his scenes of high life better with a servant girl and an orange vendor as models than with Major and Mrs Monarch, who are indubitably the real thing. The texture of the writing is simpler and the idea, which is an allegory on James's own ideas about art, need not be taken too literally in its particular instance. It is the general truth which concerned him, and he means to reveal an odd side to the artistic imagination.

James is like Proust and James Joyce in that he is one of the most autobiographical of the great fiction writers. Not that he used the actual events of his life in his writing in more than a few instances; but that his mental life, his thoughts, conflicts and emotions, found expression in his work. All novelists, of course, do this to some extent, but in James one is always conscious of it. In 'The Middle Years' he shows that same sense of disappointment which he revealed more strongly through Strether in *The Ambassadors*; he says of Dencombe, 'It had taken so much of his life to produce so little art. The art had come, but it had come after every-thing else.' There is, too, the idea of what 'might have been' in 'The Jolly Corner', in which the expatriate Spencer Brydon revisits his childhood home in New York and sees his *alter ego*, as a kind of imagined ghost, a man 'evil, odious, blatant, vulgar', corrupted by a civilization from which he himself has escaped into the tradition and gracious-ness of Europe. We have considered something of the com-plicated relationship between James and the country of his birth; this story may be taken as his final feeling about America, since it was written after the 1903 visit, following which he wrote *The American Scene*.

'The Next Time' is another autobiographical story, in

which the hero is a serious novelist whose whole career has been a series of attempts to write a vulgar best-seller; each has no more than a success of esteem. The story was written just after James's own attempt at popular success, his assault upon the theatre. In 'The Figure in the Carpet' he describes the search made for the hidden meaning in the works of a fictitious novelist called Hugh Vereker. The difference between Vereker and James is that the solution to the riddle of Vereker's meaning dies with him. No critic, it seems, has entertained the awful thought that, unknown, James's secret died with him! The whole story appears to be an allegory of the quest James intended to go on in the minds of his readers.

There is a side to James which is inherent in most of his work, but which comes out plainly in the stories; his insistence on the frustration of life, on the idea that in everybody's life there is some significant thing which he has lost or failed to achieve. 'Life is dispiriting,' he wrote in *Notes and Reviews*, 'art is inspiring, and a story-teller who aims at anything more than a fleeting success has no right to tell an ugly story unless he knows its beautiful counterpart.' And I think it is true to say that even in his ugliest stories James usually manages to convey the beautiful counterpart—so that the necessary element of pity is introduced to make his an almost 'tragic' view. To mention a few of the subjects of his stories will show in what direction his mind was preoccupied; there is Paul Overt's discovery, in 'The Lesson of the Master', that the man who has advised him, for the sake of his art, not to marry a certain girl, has taken the opportunity to marry the girl himself; Herbert Dodd's loss of a happy life through a misunderstanding; Daisy Miller's inability to know how to behave, ending in her death; there is Caroline Spencer, in 'Four Meetings,' who, having saved for the day when she will see Europe, loses her money on landing at Le Havre, and returns to America the following day; the painter Theobald, in 'The Madonna of the Future', never paints the masterpiece he constantly sees in his own mind . . . 'Frustration's only life', says Dencombe in *The Middle Years*.

The novels and the short stories form James's creative work, but his output—his 'production' as he liked to call it—was not restricted to fiction. He was a journalist, contributing reviews of books and plays to American journals, as well as a foreign correspondent, sending long travel letters with titles like 'A Roman Holiday' or 'Florentine Notes'; he was a serious critic of contemporary literature, and Mr Morris Roberts, in his book *Henry James's Criticism*, places him very high as a critic; and he was a playwright. From the end of the 'eighties until the mid-'nineties he wrote little but plays, only two of which were produced. In his correspondence he refers to his playwrighting constantly as if it were a game, through which he might make his fortune and win wide popularity as well. But it was no game; he loved the theatre passionately, as his novel, *The Tragic Muse*, shows, and the economy and perfection of form which the stage demands suited his particular genius. *The American*, adapted from his novel, had a moderate success, although the notices were on the whole 'quite awful', but it was not until the production of *Guy Domville* that he realized the public would not take to his plays. *Guy Domville* is set in the eighteenth century and is about a Catholic who is prevented from becoming a priest by being told that it is his duty to produce an heir, since he is the last of the Domvilles. The London theatre of the time, used to plays of an appalling crudity, would naturally not take to such a subject and setting with ease, and when they heard James's beautiful, but literary, dialogue they were not impressed. The gallery booed at the end, and the play was damned. The blow to James was great and he returned to writing novels and short stories. But the urge to write plays did not entirely leave him, and he wrote a few more, though with little success— see pp. 16, 17. One of these plays, *The Other House*, has a curious history. It was written as a play-scenario under the title *The Promise*, adapted as a novel in 1895, and the novel was adapted back into a play over ten years later. It is a melodrama about a woman, Rose Armiger, who murders the child of the man she loves in order to release him from his death-bed promise to his wife that, for the sake of the child, he will never marry again. It is without the 'literary' flavour of the earlier plays, with good, brisk dialogue and a mounting sense of horror which should be most effective on the stage.

As a critic of other writers his best work is to be found in *French Poets and Novelists*, published in 1878. His literary models, as a young man, had been the contemporary French writers, and he included Turgeniev among these. In this book he has his reservations about them, disliking the note of immorality which he noticed in them, but even so he would not have exchanged *Madame Bovary* for a novel of George Eliot's, whose morality he admired. The realism of the French novel appealed to him almost against his will and he says in one of his early stories, 'I have always thought the observant faculty a windy imposter so long as it refuses to pocket pride and doff its bravery and crawl on all fours, if need be, into the unilluminated corners and crannies of life'. But he would never have carried this sort of thing to Zolaesque lengths. In his essays in *The Times Literary Supplement* on 'The New Novel', published in 1914, he discusses the realistic novels of such writers as H. G. Wells, Arnold Bennett and Hugh Walpole; here again he insists on the importance of observation, on a novelist's power to 'saturate' himself in the setting of his novel. But that, he goes on to say, is not all; it is only the preparation, and it is what comes out of this, on a logic of its own, which decides the success of the novel. It is interesting to see how constant James's attitude to his art has been; in *French Poets and Novelists* he reveals what he has learnt from them, and in the later essay he is advising another generation of realistic novelists on the dangers of their path. It was H. G. Wells, in particular, who resented this advice—and even went so far as to parody James's style and attack him as an artist in his book *Boon*.

The Prefaces which James wrote to the Collected Edition of his work, in which he turns his critical mind upon himself, form his most important work of criticism. They are written in his later style and there is no denying that they are extremely difficult. All the super-subtle feelings which went into the creation of his late novels are analyzed and discussed with detachment, yet, by their nature, the prefaces are only assimilable with an understanding and knowledge of the work to which they refer. They should be read *after* reading the book.

There is no difficulty, however, in the travel sketches which he published from time to time in book form, under titles such as *A Little Tour in France*, *Portraits of Places*, or *Foreign Parts*. Their exceptional charm is in the evocation of place and atmosphere. He admits, with no trace of shame, that he is an adorer of the 'picturesque', by which he does not mean a 'picture-postcard' view, but rather the feeling by which a visual scene may produce associations with the past. He was writing for an American audience, and had no need to inhibit his Americanism, which unerringly led him to 'sentimental' feelings about tradition and the beauties of an ancient culture. But when writing about art and architecture he shows himself to have a fine visual sense, unspoilt by any pedantry. It is not uncommon to come across sentences in these articles which stand as acute art criticism; his description of a Botticelli in the Pitti Palace, for instance: ' . . . a Madonna, chilled with tragic prescience, laying a pale cheek against that of a blighted Infant.' In architectural appreciation, he says, he is always of 'the opinion of the last speaker', but this is modesty; his appreciation may be unprofessional but it is evocative in the best sense.

James wrote three books of autobiography—*A Small Boy and Others*, *Notes of a Son and Brother* and *The Middle Years*. They are not autobiography in any strict sense, although their basic structure is in the form of a memoir. They are written in the later style, and he chose to convey the 'spirit' of his life by nuance and suggestion. A quotation from *The*

Middle Years will show his method: 'To return at all across the years to the gates of the paradise of the larger initiations is to be ever so tempted to pass them, to push in again and breathe the air of this, that and the other plot of rising ground particularly associated, for memory and gratitude, with the quickening process.'

The collection of his Letters, in two volumes, gives a more explicit idea of his life. They are the letters of a charming, witty and kind-hearted man, and seem to flow 'warm from the heart and fresh from the occasion', although he must have known that they would one day appear in print and made sure that they should not shame him. Perhaps to read the letters for an hour or two is as good an introduction to James as any; their mood varies so constantly that all the facets of the man are eventually revealed.

The last few years in England have seen a great revival of interest in James. Like all great writers he went into neglect some years after his death, but now many of his books are again in print and collections of his unpublished work occasionally appear. The popularity which he so longed for during his life has at last come to him, but his direct influence on the modern English novel is not very strong. Virginia Woolf and I. Compton-Burnett learnt something from his methods, and Miss Elizabeth Bowen owes much to his technique. But he is a novelist whose effects on literature are not easily seen. He was years in advance of his time in his psychological interest in his characters; and above all, it is in its psychological content that the virtue of the modern novel may be found.

HENRY JAMES

A Select Bibliography

(Place of publication London, unless stated otherwise)

Bibliography:

A BIBLIOGRAPHY OF THE WRITINGS OF HENRY JAMES, by Le Roy Phillips; Boston (1906); new edition, New York (1930).

A BIBLIOGRAPHY OF HENRY JAMES, by L. Edel and D. H. Laurence (1957)
—a masterly work. Revised edition, 1961.

Collected Works:

COLLECTED NOVELS AND TALES, 14 vols (1883).

THE NOVELS AND TALES, 26 vols; New York (1907-9)
—with special prefaces and textual revision for vols 1-24.

UNIFORM EDITION OF THE TALES, 14 vols (1915-19).

NOVELS AND STORIES, ed. P. Lubbock, 35 vols (1921-3).

THE AMERICAN NOVELS AND STORIES; New York (1947).

FOURTEEN STORIES (1947).

THE SCENIC ART; New Brunswick (1948)
—collected papers on the theatre.

THE COMPLETE PLAYS, ed. L. Edel [1949].

THE GHOSTLY TALES; New Brunswick (1948[1949]).

THE AMERICAN ESSAYS, ed. L. Edel; New York (1956).

LITERARY REVIEWS AND ESSAYS, ed. A. Mordell; New York [1957].

THE COMPLETE TALES, ed. L. Edel. 12 vols (1962-4).

THE NOVELS, intro. L. Edel (1967—).

Selected Works:

FOURTEEN STORIES (1947).

TEN SHORT STORIES, ed. M Swan (1948).

SELECTED LETTERS, ed. L. Edel (1956).

SELECTED STORIES, ed. A Hopkins (1957)
—in the World's Classics Edition.

SELECTED LITERARY CRITICISM, ed. M. Shapira (1963).

Separate Works:

Note: The English edition alone is listed when first publication in the UK and the USA was virtually simultaneous.

A PASSIONATE PILGRIM AND OTHER TALES; Boston (1875). *Stories*

TRANSATLANTIC SKETCHES; Boston (1875). *Travel*

RODERICK HUDSON; Boston (1876[1875]). *Novel*

THE AMERICAN; Boston (1877). *Novel*

FRENCH POETS AND NOVELISTS (1878). *Criticism*

WATCH AND WARD; Boston (1878). *Novel*

THE EUROPEANS, 2 vols (1878). *Novel*

DAISY MILLER, 2 vols (1879[1878]). *Stories*

THE MADONNA OF THE FUTURE AND OTHER TALES, 2 vols (1879). *Stories*

CONFIDENCE, 2 vols (1880[1879]). *Novel*

HAWTHORNE (1879). *Criticism*

THE DIARY OF A MAN OF FIFTY and A BUNDLE OF LETTERS; New York (1880). *Stories*

WASHINGTON SQUARE, 2 vols (1881[1880]). *Stories*

THE PORTRAIT OF A LADY, 3 vols (1881). *Novel*

THE SIEGE OF LONDON; Boston (1883). *Stories*

PORTRAITS OF PLACES (1883). *Travel*

A LITTLE TOUR IN FRANCE; Boston (1885[1884]). *Travel*

TALES OF THREE CITIES (1884). *Stories*

STORIES REVIVED, 3 vols (1885). *Stories*

THE BOSTONIANS, 3 vols (1886). *Novel*

THE PRINCESS CASAMASSIMA, 3 vols (1886). *Novel*

PARTIAL PORTRAITS (1888). *Criticism*

THE REVERBERATOR, 2 vols (1888). *Novel*

THE ASPERN PAPERS, 2 vols (1888). *Stories*

A LONDON LIFE, 2 vols (1889). *Stories*

THE TRAGIC MUSE, 2 vols (1890). *Novel*

THE LESSON OF THE MASTER (1892). *Stories*

THE REAL THING AND OTHER TALES (1893). *Stories*

PICTURE AND TEXT; New York (1893). *Criticism*

THE PRIVATE LIFE (1893). *Stories*

ESSAYS IN LONDON AND ELSEWHERE (1893). *Criticism*

THEATRICALS (1894). *Plays*

THEATRICALS: SECOND SERIES (1895). *Plays*

TERMINATIONS (1895). *Stories*

EMBARRASSMENTS (1896). *Stories*

THE OTHER HOUSE, 2 vols (1896). *Novel*

THE SPOILS OF POYNTON (1897). *Novel*

WHAT MAISIE KNEW (1897). *Novel*

IN THE CAGE (1898). *Story*

THE TWO MAGICS (1898). *Stories*

THE AWKWARD AGE (1899). *Novel*
THE SOFT SIDE (1900). *Stories*
THE SACRED FOUNT (1901). *Novel*
THE WINGS OF THE DOVE, 2 vols (1902). *Novel*
THE BETTER SORT (1903). *Stories*
THE AMBASSADORS (1903). *Novel*
WILLIAM WETMORE STORY AND HIS FRIENDS, 2 vols (1903). *Biography*
THE GOLDEN BOWL, 2 vols (1904). *Novel*
THE QUESTION OF OUR SPEECH [and] THE LESSON OF BALZAC; Boston. Two Lectures. (1905). *Criticism*
ENGLISH HOURS (1905). *Travel*
THE AMERICAN SCENE (1907). *Travel*
VIEWS AND REVIEWS; Boston (1908). *Criticism*
JULIA BRIDE; New York (1909). *Story*
ITALIAN HOURS (1909). *Travel*
THE FINGER GRAIN (1910). *Stories*
THE OUTCRY (1911). *Novel*
A SMALL BOY AND OTHERS (1913). *Autobiography*
NOTES OF A SON AND BROTHER (1914). *Autobiography*
NOTES ON NOVELISTS (1914). *Criticism*
THE IVORY TOWER (1917). *Unfinished Novel*
THE SENSE OF THE PAST (1917). *Unfinished Novel*
THE MIDDLE YEARS (1917). *Autobiography*
GABRIELLE DE BERGERAC; New York (1918). *Story*
WITHIN THE RIM AND OTHER ESSAYS [1919]. *Essays*
TRAVELLING COMPANIONS; New York (1919). *Stories*
NOTES AND REVIEWS; Cambridge, Mass. (1921). *Criticism*
THE ART OF THE NOVEL: CRITICAL PREFACES (1934).
THE NOTEBOOKS OF HENRY JAMES, ed. F. O. Matthiessen and K.B. Murdock; New York (1947).
THE ART OF FICTION AND OTHER ESSAYS; New York (1948).
EIGHT UNCOLLECTED TALES; New Brunswick (1950).
THE PAINTER'S EYE. Notes and Essays on the Pictorial Arts, ed. J. L. Sweeney (1956).
PARISIAN SKETCHES, 1875-76, ed. L. Edel and I. D. Lind; New York (1957).

Letters:
THE LETTERS OF HENRY JAMES. Selected and edited by P. Lubbock, 2 vols (1920).

LETTERS OF HENRY JAMES TO WALTER BERRY; Paris (1928).

THEATRE AND FRIENDSHIP: SOME HENRY JAMES LETTERS, ed. E. Robins (1932).

HENRY JAMES AND H. G. WELLS: A RECORD OF THEIR FRIENDSHIP, THEIR DEBATE ON THE ART OF FICTION, AND THEIR QUARREL, ed. with an Introduction, by L. Edel and G. N. Ray (1958).

SWITZERLAND IN THE LIFE AND WORK OF HENRY JAMES; Berne (1966) —includes hitherto unpublished letters of James to Mrs Clara Benedict.

Some Critical and Biographical Studies:

THE NOVELS OF HENRY JAMES, by E. L. Cary; New York (1905) —the first critical book on James's work.

HENRY JAMES, by R. West (1916) —a short, sharp, and brilliant study.

HENRY JAMES: A CRITICAL STUDY, by F. M. Hueffer (1913) —an interesting, hagiographical, and not always reliable study.

THE METHOD OF HENRY JAMES, by J. W. Beach; New Haven (1918) —an excellent study of technique.

INSTIGATIONS, by E. Pound; New York (1920) —contains an essay on James.

THE CRAFT OF FICTION, by P. Lubbock (1921) —there are constant references to James throughout this work.

NOTES ON LIFE AND LETTERS, by J. Conrad (1921) —contains an appreciation of James.

READERS AND WRITERS, by A. R. Orage (1922) —contains an essay on James.

HENRY JAMES AT WORK, by T. Bosanquet (1924) —a portrait by James's secretary.

THE PILGRIMAGE OF HENRY JAMES, by Van Wyck Brooks; New York (1925) —a study of James as an expatriate novelist.

THEORY AND PRACTICE IN HENRY JAMES, by H. L. Hughes; Ann Arbor (1925).

HENRY JAMES: MAN AND AUTHOR, by P. Edgar (1927) —a careful introduction to James's work.

THE SENSE OF GLORY, by H. Read (1929) —contains an essay on James.

EARLY DEVELOPMENTS OF HENRY JAMES, by C. P. Kelley; Illinois (1930).

LES ANNEES DRAMATIQUES, by L. Edel; Paris (1931) —the only full account of James as a playwright.

THE PREFACES OF HENRY JAMES, by L. Edel; Paris (1931).

PORTRAITS, by D. MacCarthy (1931)
—contains a portrait of James.

A BACKWARD GLANCE, by E. Wharton; New York (1934)
—Mrs Wharton's autobiography, containing many references to James.

THE GEORGIAN LITERARY SCENE, by Swinnerton (1935)
—contains an essay on James.

THE THOUGHT AND CHARACTER OF HENRY JAMES, by R. B. Perry, 2 vols; Boston (1935).

THE MODERN FABLES OF HENRY JAMES, by E. M. Snell; Cambridge, Mass. (1935).

THE DESTRUCTIVE ELEMENT, by S. Spender (1935)
—contains essays on James.

THE TRIPLE THINKERS, by E. Wilson (1938)
—contains an essay 'The Ambiguity of Henry James'.

HENRY JAMES: THE MAJOR PHASE, by F. O. Matthiessen (1944)
—studies the symbolism of the later novels.

THE LEGEND OF THE MASTER, ed. S. Nowell Smith (1947)
—an anthology of reminiscences of James.

THE QUESTION OF HENRY JAMES, ed. F. W. Dupee (1947)
—a collection of essays by various hands.

THE JAMES FAMILY: A GROUP BIOGRAPHY, by F. O. Matthiessen (1948)
—a long book containing much new material.

HENRY JAMES AND THE EXPANDING HORIZON, by O. Andreas (1948).

THE GREAT TRADITION, by F. R. Leavis (1949)
—contains a study of James.

THE CROOKED CORRIDOR: A STORY OF HENRY JAMES, by E. Stevenson (1949).

LES LETTRES AMERICAINES DEVANT LA CRITIQUE FRANCAISE (1887-1917), by C. Arnavon; Paris (1952).

HENRY JAMES: THE UNTRIED YEARS, 1843-69, by L. Edel (1953)
—the first volume of a five-volume definitive biography. See *The Conquest of London*, *The Middle Years*, *The Treacherous Years*, below.

YOUNG HENRY JAMES: 1843-1870, by R. C. Le Clair; New York (1955).

THE THEMES OF HENRY JAMES, by E. T. Bowden (1956).

THE AMERICAN HENRY JAMES, by Q. Anderson (1958).

THE AMERICAN NOVEL AND ITS TRADITION, by R. Chase (1958).

HENRY JAMES, by D. W. Jefferson (1960)
—in the Writers and Critics series.

JAMES'S LATER NOVELS, by R. Marks; New York (1960).

THE COMIC SENSE OF HENRY JAMES: A STUDY OF THE EARLY NOVELS, by W. R. Poirier (1960).

A CASEBOOK ON HENRY JAMES'S 'TURN OF THE SCREW', ed. G. Willen; New York (1960).

THE HOUSES THAT HENRY JAMES BUILT, by R. W. Stallman (1961).

THE NOVELS OF HENRY JAMES, by O. Cargill; New York (1962).

THE ORDEAL OF CONSCIOUSNESS IN HENRY JAMES, by D. Krook; Cambridge (1962).

HENRY JAMES: THE CONQUEST OF LONDON, 1870-83, by L. Edel (1962)
—the second volume of the biography.

HENRY JAMES: THE MIDDLE YEARS, 1884-94, by L. Edel (1963)
—the third volume of the biography.

HENRY JAMES AND HIS CULT, by M. Geismar (1964).

HENRY JAMES AND THE MODERN READER, by D. W. Jefferson (1964).

THE BATTLE AND THE BOOKS; SOME ASPECTS OF HENRY JAMES, by E. Stone; Ohio (1964).

PLOTS AND CHARACTERS IN THE FICTION OF HENRY JAMES, by R. Gale; Connecticut (1965).

IMAGINATION AND LIVING; HENRY JAMES'S LEGACY TO THE NOVEL, by N. Lebowitz; Detroit (1966).

READER'S GUIDE TO HENRY JAMES, by S. G. Putt (1966).

PERSPECTIVES ON JAMES'S 'THE PORTRAIT OF A LADY', ed. W. T. Stafford; New York (1967).

THE SEARCH FOR FORM; STUDIES IN THE STRUCTURE OF JAMES'S FICTION, by J. A. Ward; N. Carolina (1967).

HENRY JAMES, by R. Gard (1968)
—Critical Heritage Series.

HENRY JAMES, ed. T. Tanner (1968)
—Modern Judgements Series.

STRANGE ALLOY—THE RELATION OF TRAGEDY AND COMEDY IN THE FICTION OF HENRY JAMES, by E. D. Leyburn; N. Carolina (1968).

HENRY JAMES AT HOME, by H. Montgomery Hyde (1969).

HENRY JAMES: THE TREACHEROUS YEARS, 1895-1901, by L. Edel (1969)
—the fourth volume of the biography.

INDEX OF SHORT STORIES

The title in italics refers to the volume in which the story appears

Great Condition, The, *The Soft Side*
Great Good Place, The, *The Soft Side*
Greville Fane, *The Real Thing and Other Tales*
Guest's Confession, *Travelling Companions*
Impressions of a Cousin, The, *Tales of Three Cities*
In the Cage, *In the Cage*
International Episode, An, *Daisy Miller*
Jersey Villas, as Sir Dominick Ferrand in *The Real Thing and Other Tales*
Jolly Corner, The, *Novels and Tales*, New York Edition, Vol. XVII
John Delavoy, *The Soft Side*
Julia Bride, *Julia Bride*
Lady Barberina, *Tales of Three Cities*
Landscape Painter, A, *Stories Revived*
Last of the Valerii, The, *A Passionate Pilgrim and Other Tales*
Lesson of the Master, The, *The Lesson of the Master*
Liar, The, *A London Life*
Light Man, A, *Stories Revived*
London Life, A, *A London Life*
Longstaff's Marriage, *The Madonna of the Future and Other Tales*
Lord Beaupre, *The Private Life and Other Tales*
Louisa Pallant, *The Aspern Papers*
Madame De Mauves, *A Passionate Pilgrim and Other Tales*
Madonna of the Future, The, *A Passionate Pilgrim and Other Tales*
Marriages, The, *The Lesson of the Master*
Master Eustace, *Stories Revived*
Maud-Evelyn, *The Soft Side*
Middle Years, The, *Termination*
Miss Gunton of Poughkeepsie, *The Soft Side*
Modern Warning, The, *The Aspern Papers*
Mora Montravers, *The Finer Grain*
Most Extraordinary Case, A, *Stories Revived*
Mrs Medwin, *The Better Sort*
Mrs Temperley, *A London Life*
My Friend Bingham, *Eight Uncollected Tales*
New England Winter, A, *Tales of Three Cities*
Next Time, The, *Embarrassments*
Nona Vincent, *The Real Thing and Other Tales*
Osborne's Revenge, *Eight Uncollected Tales*
Owen Wingrave, *The Private Life*
Pandora, *Stories Revived*

Papers, The, *The Better Sort*
Passionate Pilgrim, A, *A Passionate Pilgrim and Other Tales*
Paste, *The Soft Side*
Patagonia, The, *A London Life*
Path of Duty, The, *Stories Revived*
Pension Beaurepas, The, *Washington Square*
Point of View, The, *The Siege of London*
Poor Richard, *Stories Revived*
Private Life, The, *The Private Life*
Problem, A, *Eight Uncollected Tales*
Professor Fargo, *Travelling Companions*
Pupil, The, *The Lesson of the Master*
Real Right Thing, The, *The Soft Side*
Romance of Certain Old Clothes, The, *A Passionate Pilgrim and Other Tales*
Rose-Agathe, *Stories Revived*
Round of Visits, A, *The Finer Grain*
Siege of London, The, *The Siege of London*
Sir Dominick Ferrand, *The Real Thing and Other Tales*
Sir Edmund Orme, *The Lesson of the Master*
Solution, The, *The Lesson of the Master*
Special Type, The, *The Better Sort*
Story of a Masterpiece, The, *Eight Uncollected Tales*
Story in It, The, *The Better Sort*
Story of a Year, The, *American Novels and Stories*
Sweetheart of M. Brisieux, The, *Travelling Companions*
Theodolinde, *Stories Revived*
Third Person, The, *The Soft Side*
Tone of Time, The, *The Better Sort*
Travelling Companions, *Travelling Companions*
Tree of Knowledge, The, *The Soft Side*
Turn of the Screw, The, *The Two Magics*
Two Countries, as The Modern Warning in *The Aspern Papers*
Two Faces, The, *The Better Sort*
Two Magics, The, *The Two Magics*
Velvet Glove, The, *The Finer Grain*
Visits, The, *The Private Life*
Watch and Ward, *Watch and Ward*
Way it Came, The, *Embarrassments*
Wheel of Time, The, *The Private Life*